A Mollusk Without a Shell

Akron Series in Contemporary Poetics

Akron Series in Contemporary Poetics

Mary Biddinger and John Gallaher, Editors
Nick Sturm, Associate Editor
Jordan McNeil, Associate Editor

A Mollusk Without a Shell

Essays on Self-Care for Writers

Julie Brooks Barbour
& Mary Biddinger, editors

The University of Akron Press
Akron, Ohio

ISBN: 978-1-62922-279-0 (paper)
ISBN: 978-1-62922-280-6 (ePDF)
ISBN: 978-1-62922-281-3 (ePub)

A catalog record for this title is available from the Library of Congress.

The paper used in this publication meets the minimum requirements of ANSI NISO Z39.48–1992 (Permanence of Paper). ∞

The views contained herein are those of the individual authors and do not necessarily reflect the views of the editors, the Akron Series in Contemporary Poetics, or The University of Akron Press.

Cover: Illustration and cover design by Rhye Pirie.

Sarah Frelity. "Ann Arbor, 1974" from *We*, Harbor Editions, 2021, p. 9. Reprinted with the permission of Harbor Editions.

A Mollusk Without a Shell was designed and typeset in Garamond with Futura titles by Amy Freels and printed on sixty-pound natural and bound by Baker & Taylor Publisher Services of Ashland, Ohio.

Affordable Learning Initiative
THE UNIVERSITY OF AKRON

Produced in conjunction with the University of Akron Affordable Learning Initiative. More information is available at www.uakron.edu/affordablelearning/

For our students.

Contents

Introduction

Julie Brooks Barbour and Mary Biddinger

SAY WHAT YOU WILL, but a Gen X adolescence prepared us for the pandemic, especially those of us who were bookish junior goths scribbling in notebooks, flipping through our favorite zines, and listening to The Cure in solitude. Were we writers then? Perhaps, or at least we were destined to be. Did we understand how friendships can make the difference between utter alienation and steadfast camaraderie? To an extent, yes.

Decades later, one of the unexpected gifts of COVID lockdowns was the opportunity to forge friendships over distance with iPhone calls, text messages galore, and Zoom meetings where our internet connections became unstable and then stable again. This essay collection is born from one of those friendships and the desire to expand our understanding of how writers take care of themselves during challenging times. Our starting point was shared experience as late-fortysomething women writers. We looked to peers within and beyond our generation, hoping to find advice. We present this collection of ten essays as a companion for anyone who needs to protect and fortify their writer selves.

As we developed our own practices for sustaining writing—hunkered in rooms with teenage kids and cats and colleagues and noise on the other side of the door—we thought about how other writers were likely doing the same. Could we maybe ask them for insight? And while asking for insight, might we also trouble them for a writing prompt for future inspiration? To our delight, we received a robust response to our queries, and each of the essays in this collection is a bundle of wisdom and encouragement. Essayists speak of their relationship with nature, of their need to evaluate habits and create new ones, and of the importance of boundaries and understanding. Readers will find a blend of practical guidance (thank you, Charlie, for telling us about your inspiring writing ritual), humor (Kelli, we can't read a sentence of your essay without hearing your amazing voice speaking every word), music (Mixby, we are cranking Siouxsie right now and forever), and of course poetic language (Lee, thank you again for the "mollusk without a shell" that became this book's title).

While creative writing classes might teach us how to tend our poems and stories, or at least walk us through the process of germination and various draft phases, ultimately coming to some sense of completion, seldom do they address the care of the actual writer who is searching for words and putting them on the page. Sometimes we think of writing like bird watching. We sit quietly waiting for a chickadee to land, but much of that time is spent contemplating the tree or the wind that moves the branch. And how are we to care for ourselves in the meantime? Literary history offers few examples of writerly self-care, and in workshops we do not speak of it often beyond checking in with each other and briefly consoling each other during hard times.

When creating submission guidelines for the essays in this project, we asked that the contributions be brief and for writers to draw upon personal experience however they felt fit. We also asked each writer to include a prompt that could be connected to the essay, or not. Our goal in creating this volume was not to overwhelm, but to create a reference that is easy to visit and revisit. The ten essays in *A Mollusk Without a Shell* represent a vast range of experiences and approaches to writerly self-care, sharing thoughts and vulnerabilities, and perhaps most importantly, a spirit of care that permeates every piece of advice. We hope this book is as lovely a companion for readers as it has been for us during the process of bringing it into the world.

The Ritual

Charles Jensen

MY FRIEND KAREN ASKED me if I liked routines. We were walking across our college campus, probably heading toward a coffee shop where we could kill an hour or two. At the time, even the word *routine* filled me with boredom and dread. "No," I said, full of certainty. "But I do like rituals."

"What's the difference?"

"A ritual," I said, forming the thought as I spoke, "is a routine with purpose."

I associated *routine* with its worst contexts. A day-in, day-out sequence of steps that don't change, that grind down creativity and imagination into dust to be blown away by the wind. An uninspired execution of a task. An action that lacks surprise and discovery. Somehow differentiating these ideas—the mundane with something much more sublime—made the idea of repetition palatable for me.

Fast-forward twenty-five years, and the people in my life would tell you, unequivocally, that my entire life is dominated by routines. Routines I love. Routines from which I hate to deviate.

But what appears to be a routine from the outside is, to me, a ritual.

My most productive periods of writing have been informed and shaped by ritual—an unwavering commitment not necessarily to a process, but to an outcome. Writing prose lends itself seamlessly to a routine—wherever you left off the day prior, you pick up and begin again. It's as graceful as a baton handoff between relay runners, and it helps you move closer to the finish line each time.

Routines don't have to be permanent, fixed, or inflexible. With poetry, I find routines to be best employed as short sprints of productivity, maintaining a focus on a specific goal. This is why I sometimes feel writing a poem a day during April in honor of National Poetry Month (or any month I decide is a poetry month) has its own kind of magic. Not every poem is good, and not every day ends up getting a poem, but by the end of the month, I've gotten a lot. And for that routine, that's my goal: drafts. As many as possible. Raw material to rebuild from the ground up.

Even just the pressure of having to write *something* means I'm more inclined to take creative risks that wouldn't have occurred to me if I wasn't desperate. For instance, desperate for a poem one day, I took Wallace Stevens's "Thirteen Ways of Looking at a Blackbird" and wrote over it, copying the form, structure, and lineation to write "Thirteen Ways of Looking at Los Angeles." I used this idea a few more times and established a new form I call "the reboot." I never would have done it without the insistence of my routine that month. This is because the core of ritual is expectation: if I do x, the outcome will be y. If I do not do x, the outcome cannot be guaranteed to be y.

I am, for better and for worse, a morning person. Please don't stop reading. I'm not here to tell you that you should become one, or go against your natural biorhythms. But I will tell you that the morning is the only time of day I am almost certain to be able to keep to myself. No one schedules a 6 a.m. meeting with me. No household chores need to be addressed before sunrise.

I use these early hours selfishly. I wake up at 5:30 a.m. and drive to my gym, where I exercise for the better part of an hour. Then I drive home, clean myself up, and get down to writing. I work out four days a week and write for five. The fifth day—the glorious Wednesday of the week—I sleep that extra hour before writing as a treat. When I finish my hour, I move on to my paid employment work, just in time for the start of business hours.

I think locating your sacred time is critical for writing routines of all kinds.

My mother died in 2011 after a multi-year fight against cancer. At one point during those years, reflecting on her life and how she'd squirreled away every bit of spare money she could, she told my brother Gary, "Money isn't the currency of life. Time is." The words have haunted me ever since and have become such a foundational way of how I organize my life. Time is precious. We can't earn more of it. And it gets spent whether we're intentional about it or not. Therefore, be intentional.

Time is also the currency of writing. Writers never have enough of it, and we freely expend what we do have each time we sit down to work. That axiom, though, is in direct conflict with another truth: we will stretch out our work to fill the time we have to complete it. If you have four hours to complete a two-hour task, suddenly it might take you all four hours. Likewise, I know there are diminishing returns if I allow myself a solid four-hour block to work.

Eventually, I'll tire. I'll run out of ideas. Or I'll get antsy. Instead of creating opportunities for those outcomes, I eliminate them by giving myself one hour. One hour per weekday to write. With just that investment, in one month

I can have twenty or more new poem drafts. I can write a complete novel draft in sixty writing sessions. I can make meaningful progress with revisions, both marking up drafts and typing in changes. And, when other factors in my life allow, I can give more time to my writing. But I do everything I can not to give less.

I've completed a lot of work this way. The repetition has imbued this sixty-minute period of my day with all the creativity I can muster. And it's happening when I'm most awake.

More than that, though, by engaging in this ritual, I find my subconscious mind keeps working on my writing throughout the day. When I sit down for the next session, my creativity is ready. And it just goes.

This ritual has become a form of self-care. While I don't write as therapy and don't view writing as therapeutic in and of itself, I acknowledge that engaging in this writing practice has therapeutic effects on me. My mental health is better. I feel more resilient. I am often a kinder, gentler version of myself. I experience more gratitude. Paradoxically, I attribute this to putting first the things that are most important to me.

I acknowledge this is a privilege many times over and that my access to resources that allow me this freedom are not universal. As the host of *The Write Process* podcast,

I've spoken with dozens of writers about how they've completed specific projects. There is no one way. There is no right way. But the guiding principle I could identify in each conversation was that the writer *prioritized* the work, even if it came second to raising children or engaging in paid employment. When you elevate your writing practice to be among your top life priorities, it gives you permission to tend to it. Guard it. Invest in it. Because investing in your writing is, ultimately, an investment in *you*. And that investment pays off exponentially.

A ritual becomes a priority. The most important aspect of the ritual is you value it for what it is: time well spent.

Since the success of my writing ritual is going to be measured by its outcome, I developed a new element for my process. I started to document my work. I'm still exploring what this means for various projects, but it began when I started logging how many words I wrote in a given session. Over the course of sixty days as I drafted a novel, I counted and recorded. I calculated my average words per day (about 1,600). I identified my lowest count (557) and my highest count (2,259). Not every day is great, but greatness isn't the point. Progress is.

In my years of writing (I'd say *earnestly* over *professionally* since the former is my internal alignment, and the latter is how others might perceive me), I've had ups and downs, ebbs and flows. There were years I wrote at sundown, between the end of my day job and the start of my personal time; a year I wrote most of a poetry book at night in bed; years when—either due to poor choices or forces outside my control—I didn't write much at all. My writing ritual is a defense against those years when I didn't make progress. While I have specific projects I want to complete, the common denominator in my work is that I want to keep going. And the key resource I need for that is time.

The pressure I feel about my practice is generally a positive one. I don't focus on writing great literature; I just focus on writing something. Even if it's bad. Even if I think it won't see the light of day. Every act of writing, whether it ends up in print or ends up in a forgotten file on my computer, moves me closer to my goals. Over time, what starts as a habit becomes entrenched in my life, so much a part of me and how I live each day that separating myself from it feels painful.

Prompt

Choose one or both of the following options:

- Set aside time to write on a regular basis. It can be fifteen minutes; it can be 150 minutes. Whatever you have capacity to give to yourself regularly. If you have the opportunity, set a time each writing session when you will begin and end. If you can't set a time, set a circumstance, such as taking ten minutes in the car before heading to work, or during a lunch break. Then, do it.

- Keep a writing log of your accomplishments for each writing session. This can be word count, number of pages drafted, number of lines revised, number of queries sent—anything and everything has a space here. How did you use the time you spent on yourself? Write it down. Update it each time. Keep it visible in the space you write in—even if the only space you have is inside the front cover of your notebook.

Wayfinding

Jenny Sadre-Orafai

WHEN I FIRST SEE it, I think *so much green*. It's spring, and everything is just born and ready to be seen. I think *I'll never make it here* as I'm shown around the cabin. *I have to go back home.* I'm one of the last to arrive. I'm given a bell with *American Dairy Association* engraved across the front. It's suggested we wear the bells if we want to hike or walk anywhere because of the bears and their bad eyes. We receive maps of the property and are reminded that fellows are not allowed to show up unannounced at one another's studios. We are to respect space and privacy and process.

I have thirty minutes before the first dinner with the other artists and writers, and I'm certain that the dinners will be the most difficult part of the residency for me. Socially awkward and introverted, my idea of a conversation starter is asking people what band their personality would sound like. That, or what's your favorite color. I always say Goldfrapp and robin's egg blue. I know the answers to my own questions. There's a mossy log in front of the cabin in the shape of an alligator. I tell myself it's real and it's watching over me, protecting me from so much danger.

I write best in silence. A window so that I can see outside is ideal, but I can do without it if I need to. Without fail, the place where I write best is on an airplane. Someone tells me it's because I'm an air sign, and I believe it.

My spouse is an artist, and when he works, he has a movie playing in the background. Since the pandemic, there's been little quiet in our house. We both work from home. The first year, I couldn't concentrate. Not only was I not writing, but I was also unable to read. A stack of books, their spines never expanded, faced me before I fell asleep each night.

The gym shut down, so I took walks around the neighborhood—one that we had moved into a year before the pandemic. Our first house. I didn't know the streets or the houses yet. I had my phone and an app that brought me back home when I got lost.

It's a part of town that I had only driven through briefly before we moved here. I had given a reading at the library down the street twelve years earlier. There's a Garden of the

Month sign that gets passed around in the neighborhood. We celebrate what we're growing outside while we're inside. Victory gardens and signs thanking essential workers and healthcare providers can be counted on two hands.

I'm not bothered by all the moths since the residency director told me to expect their thrumming on the windows and door. I'm not even bothered by the spiders that appear in the bathroom and kitchen. Each time, I take a glass from the shelf and cup the insect against the floor and then slide a piece of paper, mostly poems, underneath their bodies and set them outside.

Still, it's the loneliest I've ever felt. I drive into town to get near a tower, and I download audiobooks. I learn I can move around more assuredly when there's someone else's voice filling up the spaces first. Maybe it's because I have a younger sister, and her company was a comfort when I was young. It tides me over until porch dinners when I get to talk with the other fellows. We laugh into wine glasses and chat about our days. One person has paint on their hands.

On my early pandemic walks in the neighborhood, I began listening to interviews with writers and poets. My eyes scanned the ground as I heard Donika Kelly talk with

Jordan Kisner about her mother and therapy and planets. Sometimes I walked during drop-off at the nearby elementary school, and I had to rewind an episode because there were too many cars and people streaming in and out. One day I was listening to Hilary Leichter talk with Alex Higley and Lindsay Hunter about how a short story turned into her novel *Temporary*, when I called a dog to me so that he wouldn't get hit by a car. He ran away and a car pulled up beside me. The driver explained that she'd been following the dog for half an hour. Another day a group of twenty teenagers in shorts rushed by me, making time. As the herd of runners glided by talking, I understood that listening to the interviews made me feel less lonely.

I'm not listening to learn. It's about paying attention and reminding myself that I'm not the only one doing this work. It's witnessing a conversation between two people who are being vulnerable with each other in a moment and in their sharing of that conversation. This serves as a model for me—someone who struggles with vulnerability. For someone who, when a stranger has bought a book of mine without my knowledge then hands it to me to sign, my face flushes immediately.

It was early in the pandemic when I listened to a fascinating and revelatory conversation between CAConrad and David Naimon. In the episode, Conrad shares their thoughts on creativity and ritual. I sent that nearly two-hour conversation to writer friends and to my family. Months later, I took a virtual workshop with Conrad. That conversation gave me a window into someone else's creative processes, and I wanted to see it and try to enact it for myself.

One afternoon some of the others leave their studios to go for a hike. I go too. We talk the whole way. It's such a relief to be outside of our cabins, our work, our heads. We talk about careers, music, and bad reality television. We take pictures of waterfalls, a snake, and each other on a suspended bridge in a sun that burns all of us a little.

When I get back to the cabin, I unclip my manuscript and hang each page side by side and into rows. They look like planted tufts of white flowers or vegetables. I walk around the cabin and watch them. I fall asleep in the bed writing, and I wake up in the bed writing until I have something I can say belongs to me. By the last morning, I've written fifty-five poems. I hang them up, rows of clothes on a line. I realize then that I need movement and conversation before I can come back to the page, to where I left off.

I don't have a method for choosing the conversation that accompanies me on my walks. It's a little like divining. I know that I'll listen to what I need to listen to. When I started writing creative nonfiction again and was feeling a little shaky since it's not my primary genre, I heard a conversation between Brad Listi and Jami Attenberg, who recently published a memoir, and she talked about what it felt like for her to write outside of fiction. When I was thinking about abandoning a project that I last worked on five years ago, I listened to a conversation about someone who started over and survived. When I felt anxious in between books, I turned to a conversation about the special energy that happens during that time. When I had a book come out during the pandemic, a conversation between Jenn Baker and Anjali Enjeti was eye-opening. When I was revising a manuscript that has family and time at its center, I heard a conversation between Vanessa Angélica Villarreal and Stacey Park that I thought about for days.

The last afternoon of the residency, I leave the cabin to meet up with another fellow, a photographer. She wants to see a bog across the road from where we meet and eat most nights. She wants to take photographs there. Black fabric drapes across her body and the camera. She rustles underneath it and shuffles film cartridges. When we get back to the car, my feet and pants are covered in mud. I hose my running shoes off at the side of the house before dinner and watch the mud wash away from the house and down into the road.

❧

I've been fortunate enough to be in conversation with other writers at conferences, at school when taking classes, at school when teaching, on airplanes, on social media, on blogs. I miss these conversations, and I'm grateful for the people who put in the incredibly hard work of reading, researching, and producing podcasts. They've saved me. As someone who never felt a part of much, I feel like I'm part of a community.

Even the act of walking is a kindness that I've shown to myself after years of overexercising–obsessively running for hours. My body broken from my time on the treadmill. In between sidestepping earthworms on concrete in the morning, I text myself ideas for manuscripts or something that I want to tell my students later. So much of being a writer and poet for me is about paying attention.

Writing is wayfinding, and these conversations have guided me back to writing and reading and back to community. I don't use the map app to get home anymore, and I don't know all the streets in the neighborhood. That's not the point really. I know that I'll end up back at my quiet desk if I keep walking and keep listening.

Prompt

Go for a walk—it can be as long or as short as you can manage—and consider the questions below. Write your way into a poem.

What can you tell us about your childhood?
What was the last portal you went through?
How would you describe your work?
What's your writing process like?
What's next for you?

Works Cited

"Anjali Enjeti." *Minorities in Publishing with Jenn Baker.* 27 May 2021.

"CAConrad: Resurrect Extinct Vibration." *Between the Covers: Conversation with Writers in Fiction, Nonfiction & Poetry with David Naimon.* 16 Dec. 2019.

"Donika Kelly." *Thresholds with Jordan Kisner.* 2 June 2021.

"Episode 754, Jami Attenberg." *Otherppl with Brad Listi.* 19 Jan. 2022.

"Hilary Leichter." *I'm a Writer But with Alex Higley and Lindsay Hunter.* 18 Nov. 2021.

"The Reality of Language: A Conversation with Vanessa Angélica Villarreal." Poets at Work. 9 June 2020.

This Distractable Life
Trying to Be Engaged in a World Longing for Your Attention

Kelli Russell Agodon

IF THERE WAS A handbook for self-care during the pandemic, mine would have been called *How to Eat Smoked Cheese in Bed: A Memoir*. In challenging times, some of us gain momentum, seize the moment, and start our own reality show about remodeling the bathroom, and some of us sit on the couch with a blueberry smoothie watching *RuPaul's Drag Race*. I was the second human in that sentence. But along with cheering for my favorite drag queens and keeping the smoked gouda companies in business, I realized that besides cheese and smoothies, when things get rough, I reach for poetry.

As a poet, *self-care* can be one of those concepts that looks good on paper, but is rarely given much attention (especially when it's most needed)—sort of like buying a table lamp with a gorgeous stained-glass peacock lampshade, but never turning it on and sitting in the dark for hours. These are the times I experience such an "overwhelmedness" with life; I may not know what I need until I find myself going a little 1960s Timothy Leary and *turning on, tuning in, dropping out.*

In these times, I replace larger arenas (such as the internet or social media) with smaller simpler spaces that include books, writing, and naps. Though several times when I most needed self-care, I didn't realize it until I found myself stepping out of the shower, putting on my robe, and instead of getting dressed—heading directly back to bed with a book. These are the moments when my body and soul speak loudest with their actions to my mind that is organizing her To Do list and ignoring her own needs.

Strangely, there are also rare times I get lucky and fall directly into self-care. When quarantine began, I made a date with a couple of friends to write poems for two hours on Zoom. Because it was so enjoyable, we made another date the next week, and then for the next year, we met every Thursday evening during the pandemic. Our "Thursday Night Poetry Club" was the self-care I needed, though had it not been for the pandemic or happened so organically, I'm not sure my working mind would have realized this was what I needed or intentionally created this space for art. Sometimes self-care is allowing new routines to fall into place by acknowledging their helpfulness.

In "normal" times (in quotes because what is "normal" these days?), for me, much of self-care is finding the luxury in daily life, whether it's in a comfy chair writing in my bullet journal, taking notes for a poem, slipping into a bubble bath before bed, or buying olives, rosemary almonds, and a nice bottle of red wine to enjoy with a friend while watching the sunset—though the key for me as an introvert is remembering I *have* friends and I'm not this untethered raft drifting through a very large ocean alone. It feels a bit cliché and a little Thoreau/Waldenesque to say, but slowing down and being present by focusing on the moment (and getting offline and tossing my computer into the metaphorical pond) is the best way I can care for myself.

My best self-care is when I'm paying attention to life's details—the purple flowers growing in the cobblestones, the small shoe left on the park bench, how my neighbor listens to Glenn Miller when he washes the El Camino he's owned since he was a young man. It's the days I wake up and read a poem to start the day, the joy of a hot shower, or opening the front door in early spring to hear the first robins of the season. It's choosing to walk under a crescent moon or warming up banana bread in the toaster to have while I skim through the magazines on the coffee table instead of jumping on social media or slipping onto the internet like a bodiless head who isn't thinking *do I really want to be doing this?* then letting corporations have their way with me—*Hey you, poet who should be writing a poem, did you know you may have crepey skin (and there's a cream for that!).* Or *I think you may need a new pair of joggers or a purse that magically turns into a therapist—click here baby, we can improve your life!* When I'm aware that the new charlatans are the screens in front of my face, I work to remove these interruptions and try to interact as an engaged poet in the world, not the distracted bystander fiddling with her phone and believing that a new pair of shoes will change her life.

Case in point—the other day during a windstorm, our neighborhood lost power. I had been frantically trying to get things done, but when the internet shut off, the day felt long, as if I had endless time. It reminded me how hours can be lost in endless scrolling, trying to respond to email, or thinking—*I am going to finish my essay on self-care today!* but instead I end up reading an article about celebrities' lesser-known siblings (Um, did you know Brad Pitt has a younger brother named Doug? It's true, and if I can get that into a poem, the time will have felt useful, otherwise, I can hear Mary Oliver asking me, *Now is this really how you want to spend your one wild and precious life? Reading clickbait?)* Oh, Mary, this distractable life I fall prey to—I so hear you!

There is a photo I saw of a man sitting on a boat looking at his phone while a humpback whale passes by below him.

He doesn't see it because something on his magic rectangle seemed more important than what was happening in the present moment. As a poet and human, I think of this photo a lot. And I get it. How many things have I missed because I was sucking up tweets like some sort of sweet milkshake I wanted to fill me up when what I needed was the nourishment of time with a friend or a book? Like everything, it's easy to overindulge in a news cycle that rolls 24-7 or follow trending topics as if there won't be twenty new trending topics tomorrow—all which must be clicked (*Did some D-list celebrity just die or say something inappropriate?—we must click to know!*) Or not. Or we can decide, I've had enough of an internet that arrives at the front of my house in a creepy white van trying to lure me in with its weird candy. Insert poetry. Insert art. Insert mindfulness.

On my best days, I realize the online world takes away from writing and my IRL world—and that I do not need to speak in acronyms (as I just did), tweet what's on my mind, take a photo of my spicy tuna rolls to share on Instagram, or even check Facebook to see who has done what. It's knowing the larger online community is there, but not relying on them for validation or likes. Self-care is allowing my everyday life to be enough and doing something (anything!) that doesn't require a couch and the glow of a laptop in my face. It's picking up a book of poems, going for a walk, and turning off the news that shoots through the screen like small daily daggers into my heart. It's saying no to what media is trying to force-feed me, and saying yes to the sustenance around me in my own landscape.

If you were to find me truly living my one wild and precious life, you'd see my self-care is writing poems, lying in a hammock on a warm summer day and watching the clouds change shape until the moon rises over the Cascade mountains. There are few things that make me feel as thankful and alive in the world than looking up at the sky—I swear, it's why there are so many moon poems! As poets, so many of us are taken by the universe spinning above our heads. And when you give the world your attention, it gives back—in feeling connected, in images for your art. The happiest and most fulfilling moments in my life never included a screen, social media, or the word *email*; they happen when I hear a heron's squawk while watching hummingbirds darting between fuchsia plants. This may be my favorite type of therapy—the days when I find the time to walk to an empty beach and read a book of poems with my feet in the sand and my back against the driftwood.

There are many times when we have to do the "thing" (go to work, pick up the kids, etc.)—but we do have moments when we can choose what we do with our time. I value the moments when I don't go down the TikTok rabbit hole and instead turn off all devices and sit down to write a poem. It hasn't been that long since we all weren't *so* connected, so I work to find the space to care for the part of me who sees the internet as the bad friend who wants me to try the beer bong because it's so much fun until it isn't, until I feel bad, and realize that well, there's three hours I'll never get back.

But in understanding I'm in charge of how I use my time, it's also important to point out I'm also understanding that I'll never catch up—I'll never get it all done, I'll never have the organized closet or inbox zero, and I'm okay with my unfinished life. I just keeping trying to choose what matters to me, whether it is writing, family, friendship, travel, something else. Even when everything feels terrible, I remind myself there is always something to be thankful for and there is material for my poems if I just pay attention. And I've learned in difficult times, it's wise to turn to poetry. Though let's be honest, in non-difficult times, it's wise to turn to poetry then, too.

Prompt

Turn off all your devices—cell phone, Wi-Fi, smart-watch, Alexa, or anything that could distract you—and find a place to sit (outside is preferable if the weather isn't too hot, cold, or wet, but inside works also). For five to ten minutes, write down what you see around you—and be specific. For example, if you see flowers in a vase write "pink stargazer lilies lean like falling fireworks from the copper ice bucket" or if you see a cloud in the sky you may write "a cloud in the shape of a giraffe" or "the giraffe cloud shifts into a brontosaurus while a song sparrow sings." Write down as many details as you can of the world around you until you have fifteen or more images to work with.

Once you have a list of images, write a poem that has nothing to do with these images, such as getting a divorce, finding a $20 bill on the street, falling in love for the first time. As you write, bring in as many specific images as you can either as metaphors or similes or as a way to ground your reader in your poem.

If you need a place to begin, consider: *Most nights, I…* or *Most days, I….* You can also begin your poem with *I remember*, then delete those words once your poem gets flowing.

Unshelled

Lee Ann Roripaugh

SOMETIMES WHEN YOU'RE FEELING some kind of way, you describe it as being like a mollusk without a shell. More often than not, it's about the acid reflux of trauma: an evocation of feeling vulnerable and raw to the point of distress, of the ways in which your hypervigilance and hypersensitivity frequently leave you overloaded, overwhelmed, overstimmed. It's a feeling of being all open wound when everything that surrounds you is salt.

The only thing to do for it, you've found, is to hide. To secrete your body into the safe shell of your apartment, let your consciousness retreat somewhere outside your body, and just wait for it to pass.

It's not what you would describe as a fugue state, per se, but it's nonetheless an abandonment, an absenting, a kind of disassociation from the body and its constant vulnerabilities: its illnesses, its pains, its chemical imbalances, its manufactured shames. It's as if the self retreats to a cartoon thought bubble above the body. Meta. Away. Safe.

You understand this is possibly an anachronistic coping mechanism, but lately you've become increasingly aware this is also the same mental space in which you *write*. Was this something you discovered as a child, growing up in an abusive household? Your consciousness absenting a body that was always wrong, safe in a room behind a closed door, free to expand, wander, daydream, and play? The sovereignty of it. The escape of it.

It's the first time you've conceptualized this space as being multi-use. Like a time-share condo! And yes, it encompasses the multiple shades of *retreat*. Retreat as in to back away from immediate danger or violence. Retreat as in solace, replenishment, nourishment. Retreat like an artist's residency. Re-treat as in to give oneself a treat, again.

You love this quiet, disembodied space where you're all thought. All dream. All possibility. As an introvert, maybe this is where you're most comfortable? And even if this is the same space where your traumatized self absents itself to, it's also the space your best self fills with daydreaming, music, language. Something like Robert Duncan's "place of first permission" from his poem "Often, I Am Permitted to Return to a Meadow."

You understand there's a contradiction here: feeling violently and nonconsensually unshelled by trauma, as opposed to being able to lay down the aching burden of too much armor—the tricky mediations of too much shell. The common denominator, perhaps, lies in the state of vulnerability, rawness, openness. Which can be either a wound, or an aperture.

Maybe because you know what it's like to come *unshelled*, you're fascinated by different types of shelled organisms. Snails, hermit crabs, armadillos. When you google the term "happy as a clam" to find out its origins, you discover that, like many clichés, it's been truncated from its full phrasing, which is "happy as a clam at high tide." Meaning that at high tide, clams are burrowed into their sandy shallows, safe from being wrested out by clam diggers and other natural predators. And so it's not even really so much a kind of *happiness* as it is a respite from feeling *preyed upon*, a period of time in which a clam can remain *unmolested*.

Lately, your time-share system seems to have completely broken down, though. Too many clamoring, demanding, and wounded selves have retreated from the overwhelming din of the present moment and are occupying your mental sanctuary all at the same time, making it impossible for the writing self to think. The traumatized self curls into the space like an oversized fetus—systematically sucking all of the oxygen from the room. Then there's the to-do-list self, who's absented the disaster zone of the body and retreated to higher ground to make sure the whole enterprise stays afloat from a safe distance. The to-do-list self who flips on like an emergency off-site generator and coolly extracts tasks from a body that miraculously continues to shamble about like some kind of automata. *You hit your marks,* you repeatedly keep telling yourself, as if this is some kind of achievement, as opposed to being the lowest possible bar.

And admittedly, it's been the *shittiest* of timelines. Several months after Trump takes office, you're diagnosed with cancer and undergo a complete hysterectomy, salpingo-oophorectomy, radical trachelectomy, and lymphadectomy. Eight weeks after your surgery, your mother, who's refused to speak to you for three years, who's said that you're no longer her daughter, calls to say your father has fallen and broken his hip, that he's in the hospital. She's alone in the house and helpless, so you go to Wyoming to take care of her and to make arrangements for your father's recovery. Shortly after your arrival, you discover that your father has had an undiagnosed stroke and is suffering from vascular dementia. When your father finally returns home from rehab later that fall, your parents systematically undo all of the caregiving, transportation, and assistive arrangements you've spent all summer setting up for them. Ultimately, your parents are identified as vulnerable, your father no longer competent, and so you must file for legal guardianship of your father and move your parents into assisted living.

You do all of this in a fog of intense, chronic pain as your severe spinal stenosis becomes increasingly debilitating. Every morning there are grueling hours of back spasms, and when you first wake, you can't walk upright. Searing electricities slice through your extremities, like hot knives through butter. Sometimes there's a numb gray static, like television fizz, signaling that your legs are about to disappear from beneath you. Every movement, every task becomes a calculation around the mathematics of pain. Pain, too, can be a kind of unshelling—erasing the intellect and leaving the raw meat of the body exposed.

On New Year's Day of 2019, your father falls at the assisted living center, suffers a catastrophic cerebral hemorrhage, and dies. You return to Wyoming to take care of the legal and logistical issues and to be with your mother, whose cognition is rapidly deteriorating. When you take her to the doctor, it's confirmed that she has Alzheimer's. You file for legal guardianship for your mother and stay in Wyoming for as long as you are able, then return to South Dakota just in time to have spine surgery.

It takes almost a full year for you to finally start to find a kind of familiar equilibrium following your father's death and your recovery from surgery. You're in the midst of a hectic series of readings to support your most recent book in spring 2020, when, like the other shoe dropping, news of a novel coronavirus becomes increasingly insistent, then increasingly dire.

You think of what happens next as a kind of *volvation*: the ability to roll oneself up into a protective ball when scared and/or threatened by predators. Giant Madagascan pill millipedes (*Glomeris pustulata*); woodlice, also known as pill bugs (*Armadillidiidae*); four-toed hedgehogs (*Atelerix albiventris*); and La Plata three-ringed armadillos (*Tolypeutes matacus*) all practice volvation.

You love the word *volvation*. And you're delighted, in particular, by the photos of three-ringed armadillos folding themselves up into water-tight balls, a clever origami, heads and tails neatly tucked in, like a feat of engineering ingenuity. In your conceptualization of volvation, it's not simply a physical defense mechanism, but a psychological defense mechanism as well. Sample sentence: In spring 2020, you volvate and neatly disassociate. Who knows where you've gone? Like a Japanese puzzle box. You imagine fiddling with the sliding pieces, the secret drawers, the patterned unlockings of the self. But you stubbornly refuse to crack back open again.

And why would you? It's a timeline checkered with psychological landmines and interconnected triggers. Having to preside over the late-stage wreckage of an abusive family not only raises personal remembrances of lack of safety, a complete lack of bodily autonomy, but these resurfacing vulnerabilities also intersect with the atrocities of the contemporary moment. It's the *nonconsensuality* of it all. The refusals to wear a mask to prevent the transmission of COVID. The refusals to get vaccinated to prevent the transmission of COVID. The incessant gun violence, the bodies riddled with bullets. The ubiquity of rape with impunity and without accountability. The plundering of natural resources. These are the penetrative violences of rape culture. These are the extractive violences of empire.

And to take in all of this awfulness while remaining fully present seems like the most hideous kind of *rawdoggery*. So you seal yourself up and let the tiny, needling stressors ping dull little sparks of anxiety against your armor while you keep dealing with what's in front of you: the work, the overcommitments, the guardianship of your declining mother. You try to repress the things that aren't within your control, and you play a relentless game of Whac-A-Mole while the world burns. But still, it's *so fucked up*. This gaslit pressure to continue on as if everything is normal. (Also nonconsensual! Also extractive!) You think that there's a toll, there *must* be a toll, in trying to survive a time that's so cataclysmic, so disruptive, without the ability to process, to grieve, to take a breath and acknowledge how changed everything is, and must be.

Extroverts are always saying that shy people need to *come out of their shells*. Why? Why this wish for obligatory unshelling that makes one vulnerable to predation, or consumption? It doesn't seem like a coincidence that *clams* are slang for *dollars*. That clams are considered something delicious to be stubbornly plundered from their shells, to be pried out of their bivalves gripped shut by surprisingly strong musculature. *Happy as a clam!*

Yet your survival as a writer depends upon a delicate balance of both *presence* and *absence.* You've always been extremely shy, extremely introverted, and the pandemic has heightened all of this to the point of social anxiety. As COVID restrictions loosen and you try to forcibly pour the self back into the body, it's shocking! To fully inhabit one's own body again feels like an uncomfortable and unpleasant process of stuffing the self back into a too-small sack. Like wrestling a futon into a new cover. A grinding awareness of software and hardware. The awkwardness of face and interface. An overwhelming and overstimming sense of presence, of feeling much too raw in the present. Where have you been? Where did you *go?*

Your self is not the same. Your body is not the same. A rejoinery that's both awkward and difficult. You feel like the creepy spectacle of the hermit crab who's poured itself into an abandoned doll head, laboriously dragging it along the beach in the viral YouTube video.

You wonder if this painful (re)integration of (re)occupying your own body is somehow a microcosm of what it might mean to be fully present in and fully (re)integrate, as human beings, into an abandoned and failing planet?

The trick of it, it seems to you, is to somehow sort out the difference between *retreat* and *retreat.*

Unvolvation: Since COVID, it seems like you've been *in retreat*, but now you are *on retreat.* For ten weeks, you've been given the gift of an artist residency in Taos, New

Mexico, in mountains and clouds. Sometimes a coyote pads through the trees outside your window at dusk.

There are still fires. There is still COVID. Mass shootings continue unabated. Roe v. Wade has just been overturned. Your frail mother continues to fall in the middle of the night at her assisted living center, breaking parts of herself: a fractured wrist, cracked ribs. But you are trying to unclench. You are trying to recalibrate a balance between presence and absence, between shelled and unshelled, and this respite is everything—this defined space away from the everyday world, this borrowed shell that exists purely for your writing self. For now, it is high tide, and for now you are going to try to be as "happy" as a clam.

Prompt

Write a poem that comes from a place of being profoundly *unshelled*, whatever that might mean for you. As you write and revise, consider if there are elements of presence and absence, like shade and sunlight, that inform you as you write the poem, or that enter into the frame or the shell of the poem itself. Are there metaphorical shells that become a part of the poem and are they structures that create form and safety, or are they maladaptive coping strategies? Are there frictions that arise between rawness and grit? Consider the relationship between form and content: is the poem a borrowed shell, like the hermit crab, or organically generated from the self/body? What are the formal and thematic tensions, troubling parasitisms, and/or beneficial symbiotic relationships (i.e., mutualism, commensalism), that arise from these interchanges between form and content?

Works Cited

Duncan, Robert. "Often I Am Permitted to Return to a Meadow." *The Opening of the Field*. New Directions, 1960, p. 7.

A Poet's Place

Abayomi Animashaun

AT THE CLOSE OF AWP a while back, I took a bus to the airport with several writers and had the luck of sitting beside a poet I admire and with whom, over the years, I'd formed some acquaintance. By that, I mean when we see each other there's an acknowledgment of sorts. And for me, it's a minor detail that to this day he can't pronounce or even remember my name.

On the bus, we engaged in the kind of trivial banter people have in elevators with one- or two-word answers. "How are you?" "Fine." "Fine weather we're having." "Great weather."

But somehow in that twenty-minute bus ride, we pushed past niceties and for a minute or so talked honestly about work. He made the transition by asking about my studies.

"Where are you now?"

At the time, I was working on my PhD at the University of Kansas. So I said, "Kansas."

"And what are you working on now?"

"Oh I don't know! I have a manuscript that feels ready. But when it comes to these things, I'm never sure. I felt good about it a year or so ago. And here I am still…"

"This is your second collection, right?"

"Yes."

"What's it called again?"

"I'm not sure, I'm torn between *Sailing for Ithaca* and *Leaving the*…"

He didn't let me finish. He burst into a long laugh. Teared. Wiped his face. Begged apologies. Tried containing himself. Swelled. And broke open laughing again.

Looking around the bus, I could see a young woman wearing headphones staring out the window. An elderly man wearing a name badge from the conference was asleep. The last person, a young man (also with a name badge from the conference) looked on, listening with interest at the unfolding conversation between me and the poet.

By this time, my poet friend had contained himself but was still smiling a *knowing* smile. The kind that says, *been there done that*. Or, *if only you'd listen to me*.

I tried guessing at what had been so funny and before I could ask, he said through more measured laughs, "Okay Odysseus. Okay Odysseus."

Then it occurred to me that he felt my reference to Ithaca was my attempt, as a young poet, to puff up my work and make myself sound important.

"I understand that the use of classical references, especially in a young writer's work, is dangerous," I said. "He risks being sophomoric..."

"Yes, you can't do that, Odysseus."

At this point, the bus pulled into his terminal, and he started to leave.

I thanked him for his suggestions, and I said I hoped he had a fine time at AWP. As the bus moved slowly from the curb, he yelled, "Bye Odysseus! Bye Odysseus!!"

By the time I got to my terminal and boarded my plane, I was deflated. And I couldn't stop thinking that I should have kept my big mouth shut.

I nursed my wound for weeks. And toyed with the idea of tossing out the manuscript—a manuscript that had taken over seven years to compile.

I slept poorly, haunted by the thought of being a fake for reading and referencing classics.

The poet's comments and reaction temporarily halted my capacity to work freely. I plunged into reexamining not just my poetics but also my identity.

And I wondered if the poet would have been so dismissive had I referenced Chinua Achebe or Lagos, even though both feature prominently in the collection.

I became a shadow of myself. And I watched as my daily routine lost verve and became "routine." My habit of waking up in the early morning to write deteriorated into waking up whenever I could and doing nothing after. I showed up to classes. Graded papers. Attended student conferences, but something inside of me had gone quiet.

At home, I was present but barely there. My wife, used to my mood swings over poetry, let it play out. Day after day, she'd leave me as I remained lost in thought on the couch for hours.

I went over the conversation again and again, and I kept coming back to "if only he'd given me two minutes to explain myself."

But what could I have said in those two minutes that would have convinced the well-regarded poet that I wasn't showing off?

That, as an immigrant, my imagination is fragmented? That I was introduced to the classics as a child in Nigeria? That within me, Sappho is as prominent as Soyinka? That there are aspects of Homer's epic that resonate with me as an immigrant in a foreign country?

The conversation wouldn't have gone far, and those two minutes of explaining myself would have left the poet unconvinced.

In "Uncertain in the Wild Frontier," I talk about my approach to poetry during my MFA years and the long road it took for me to arrive at *unknowing* as a chief mechanism of my imagination.

I look back on those years now and realize that one of the ways I displayed *certainty* was in classrooms, during workshops, where I'd try my darndest not to laugh at poems that were abstract, inaccessible, or nonrepresentational.

At the time, I felt those poems were the height of pretentiousness.

And, during classes or at the bar with friends, I wasn't shy about making clear that the sooner the poets in question got their heads out of their highfalutin asses the sooner they could begin the true work of poetry.

I expressed this sentiment openly and often without regard for how the poets in question might feel, without asking what they were trying to do, who their influences were, with whom they were trying to have conversations, and *how* they were trying to have those conversations.

That was years ago!

I have since completed MFA and PhD programs. And I now work at a university where I teach both graduate students and undergrads.

And I have come to realize that, as a poet *and* as a teacher, it is not my place to trample upon any student's (or anyone's) poems, attempts at poetry, or choice of poetics.

Moreover, it *is* my job to show students, who are impatient and overly sure of themselves, the necessary compassion I was shown when I was a student and held strong beliefs on subjects of which I knew little, often confusing passion with knowledge on the issues.

Which brings me back to my second collection.

I knew after compiling *Sailing for Ithaca* that I would *get it* in some quarters. I knew some would grumble or dismiss the book—"Oh big shot he thinks he is; he is drawing from Homer!"

In the end, I had to decide if I was writing to *please* or writing to partake of a conversation larger than myself, in order to better understand myself. The decision was easy.

Works Cited

Animashaun, Abayomi. "Uncertain in the Wild Frontier." *The Writer*, Apr. 2016.

Prompt

All poets have writers who speak to them, whose musings act as signposts as they journey from poem to poem. However, to better take part in the larger conversation, it's sometimes necessary to read beyond our natural influences, to spend time with poets who don't speak to us, to understand how their poems come about and why, in order to grow and arrive at unexpected insights. This consideration is at the heart of the following two-part exercise—the third part is optional.

1. For one week, read a poet who does not speak to you. If you're struggling with their poems, read interviews, reviews, and conversations about the poet and their poems. In your journal describe what you appreciate about the poet's work.

2. In the second week, write a series of imitation poems in the manner of the aforesaid poet. In your journal, reflect on the writer's style and discuss what you find intriguing, writing like they do. Might some of the writer's approaches to poetry be beneficial to you?

3. (Optional) Memorize one poem by this writer.

Awake
Sarah Freligh

FOR TOO MANY YEARS, I ran on cans of Tab poured warm over ice and on cigarettes—lots and lots of cigarettes. I smoked all the time and everywhere: in airports and on airplanes, at home and at work, in elevators and movie theaters and in restaurants both before and after dinner and sometimes during if the coursing was slow. I lit up whenever I was hungry until I wasn't hungry anymore, smoked until I could skim into a pair of size five jeans even on fat days. In every photo of me from that era, a cigarette protrudes like a sixth digit from the cup of my right hand.

One day at work I took the stairs from the fourth to the fifth floor and had to stop halfway up to catch my breath. It was an epiphany, a moment of *aha*. I realized that while my hair was still glossy and my skin was good, I was cindering my lungs, killing myself from the inside out. I realized that I would have to quit or die, and I knew death from emphysema to be slow and awful and hardly the stuff of springtime meadows in the cigarette commercials.

I also realized that I didn't want to quit.

At the time, there was no nicotine patch I could slap on my upper arm, no gum to chew away the cravings that gnawed at me with their sharp little teeth whenever I went cigarette-free for more than fifteen minutes. There was only a group of people that met weekly in the basement of a church and spent an entire hour talking about how we'd rather scoop out our eyeballs with a rusty spoon than endure a single minute without a cigarette. More often than not, this approach backfired, and we lit up the second we stepped out the door.

My first meeting, I remember sitting next to a fortyish couple, a man and a woman wearing expensive ski jackets and designer boots, who admitted they'd kicked heroin some years before but were now feeling powerless to quit smoking. I remember, too, filling out a questionnaire that would help predict my success at quitting, how I paused for a long time before answering a question that asked how long I waited to light up my first cigarette of the day.

I answered truthfully: I don't wait. Rather, I stayed in bed, propped an ashtray on my chest, and lit up. I smoked the cigarette down to the filter and only then could I finally put my feet on the floor and get on with my day.

My prognosis for quitting, as it turned out, was very poor.

The wisest tip that was passed on to me is that smoking isn't just one habit but many habits; once I started to understand where and why I was smoking, I could start to quit, a habit at a time. I cut out the morning-with-ashtray-in-bed ritual first and quit lighting up after meals and in my car. Eventually, I was able to quit smoking at work and finally, finally managed to go without a smoke in a bar, though I do admit to bumming a few cigarettes from strangers when the cravings got too awful. Even now, years later, I still dream that I'm smoking, and it's always in a noisy bar, always with a lot of people, and even in the dream, I rationalize it away as being "only one cigarette" until I wake up and realize that I don't smoke and haven't for years. But it's odd: for a few seconds after I wake up, I smell smoke.

For a month or so after I started to quit, I felt like I'd been beaten with a baseball bat. Everything hurt—my knees, my ankles, even my wrists and elbows, and oddly, the little finger on my left hand. The doctor said it was best to go cold turkey, but I didn't like turkey, cold or not. Exercise was prescribed, the old "use it or lose it" maxim. Jog, the doctor advised. Or walk. Which was like telling someone with no shoes to pull themselves up by the bootstraps. I couldn't walk ten feet on my sore knees. Also, it was possible to walk and smoke.

What about swimming? the doctor said. She was chirpy and positive. That's another thing about quitting smoking:

there are days when you want to slap someone, often the very people who are trying to help you.

I started swimming young, lessons at the old YMCA where the pool was hardly bigger than a bathtub and two feet deep in the shallow end. I learned how to breathe and kick, how to catch the water with my hand and pull it toward me. I was small and fast, a sprinter. My time for the fifty-yard freestyle in seventh grade was the second- or third-best in the state of Michigan. But becoming a great swimmer is like writing or playing the violin: it takes practice, years and years of a single-minded devotion that was unfathomable to me at that time. I didn't love it enough to want to do only that. I was too young to marry something I didn't know very well, and so I limited my swimming to dips on hot days, maybe a lap or two to cool off, and a cigarette afterward.

I went back to swimming because—I rationalized—it was impossible (even for me) to light up in the middle of a lap. I joined the Central YMCA in Philadelphia, which is an upscale hotel now, but back then it was where you went if you worked or lived in Center City. The pool was located in the basement, down a few flights of stairs from the locker room. It was narrow and stunk of chlorine and was always crowded, but I loved it, loved that I didn't ache, loved feeling like I was weightless even as I was putting on weight now that I wasn't goosing my metabolism with jolts of nicotine. Also, I could taste food again, and everything tasted delicious—cream-filled doughnuts from a bakery a few blocks from my apartment and Geno's cheese steaks at midnight. My bathing suit got tighter as I packed on pounds, but it was all good in the water. I was like a bar of soap, and when I was too tired to swim, I floated.

As a sportswriter, I traveled a lot and my Y membership allowed me to swim as a guest at any Y in the country. I tried to get up early, before my workday started, and head out for a swim—to the historic West Side Y in New York City with its gorgeous, tiled pool during the weeks when I covered the US Open Tennis Tournament or at the Y in Las Vegas, an oasis of calm that felt light years away from the pulse and glitz of the Strip. Once, while covering a tennis tournament in Dallas, the nice clerk at the hotel drew me a map to a Y that was within walking distance. I remember standing across the street from a red brick building waiting for a light to change when I was struck by an odd case of déjà vu: I knew this place, I'd been here, stood here, though I never had. It turned out the building was the Texas Book Depository, the building from which Lee Harvey Oswald shot and killed President John F. Kennedy. When I looked left, I could see the grassy knoll down a hill a little ways, and I felt time bending, the past reaching around to touch the present.

I settled into a routine, three or four swims a week. I swam in a couple of races in the Atlantic Ocean where the prize was a hot dog fresh from the grill and a cold can of beer. I swam through moves and rejections, layoffs and deaths of loved ones, human and animal. I cried in the water. I craved swims now instead of cigarettes—an emotion that Julie Otsuka, a former recreational swimmer herself, captures so exactly in her novel *The Swimmers*:

> And even though we do our best to resist the urge to descend—*It'll pass*, we tell ourselves—we can feel our panic beginning to rise, as though we were somehow missing out on our own lives. *Just a quick dip and everything will be all right.* (16)

In Otsuka's novel, a series of cracks shuts down the pool, exiling The Swimmers back to the real world. In March 2020, the pandemic arrived, and New York State shut down nearly everything—libraries, restaurants, movie theaters, health clubs, schools, and swimming pools. Groceries and liquor stores stayed open. Both were essential and often the only time I talked to an actual someone. I walked a lot, watched the grass turn from brown to green, watched crocuses and daffodils and then tulips poke up and out, but the world stayed shut down, quiet. I got used to wearing a strip of cloth across my nose and mouth, got used to veering around people on the sidewalk. I missed water, missed the person I was when I was in the water, moving through the water, and then I felt guilty about missing the water when so many people were ill and dying. I went to bed at night and felt my heart fist my chest. Mornings I watched the sun come up and did it all again.

I spent far too much time on the Internet staring at pictures of water—rivers and lakes and oceans—and the people who swam in them. I was especially drawn to a hardy group of people in the UK who dipped year-round wherever they could and in whatever weather, people of various ages and shapes and fitness levels. Wild swimmers, they called themselves. They even had a virtual group, The Outdoor Swimming Society, whose purpose is to "provide a space within which a community of independent spirits can share the joy and adventure of swimming outdoors" (Outdoor Swimming Society website). Research suggests the "joy" found in cold-water swimming isn't just emotional, but has physical benefits, too. Cold water boosts the immune system, improves circulation, and activates endorphins, providing a natural high. The people in the pictures did indeed look joyful. I wanted to be wild and joyful instead of anxious and cooped up inside myself. I needed to swim again.

In late April, on a day when the sun came up high and hot, I drove six miles north and waded into Lake Ontario. The water temperature was still in the fifties, so cold it stung, but I swam for about ten minutes. I did it again the next day and the next, each day a few minutes longer. The knotted fist that I'd carried in my stomach since the start of the pandemic loosened when I was in the water. I was away from the world, away from people and the virus that was fogging the world, and I was swimming again. I got to know the dogs and their walkers and the few other swimmers— a fit couple in wetsuits, a woman who water-walked for three hours, and a guy who did yoga poses in shallow water. We rarely spoke, but I felt like I knew those people, understood their need for water. Like me, they were swimmers. *Just a quick dip and everything will be all right.*

One early morning in mid-August, I waded into the water in the dark and watched the sun rise. I was alone out there, but it felt okay. I was swimming. I felt safe.

Woohoo, I said.

A plane droned overhead. I could hear the traffic on the lake road pick up. The world was waking up, heading for wherever. *Woohoo*! I said again, louder this time. I was already awake.

Prompt

I often think of writers as miners of the past. We persist in tapping away at stubborn walls of memory in order to expose the vein of gold we're sure is there, the people and places and objects that made up a certain time and, in doing so, hope that what we find will shed light on how we got from there to here.

My poem—"Ann Arbor 1974" (Freligh 9), travels back to a specific event and time and attempts to recreate that time and place for the reader in sensory and significant detail.

Ann Arbor, 1974

Sky bruising purple when I stuck out
my thumb and caught a fast ride
west in a spoke-wheeled Cadillac
with three geezers who passed
a silver flask of Scotch, honeyed
with age, and even I sang along
with Sinatra on the car stereo, soprano
blanketing their reedy tenors, all the way
to South Bend where the driver
handed me a Hershey bar and a wad
of ones. I played pinball for hours
at the Greyhound station, high
on horsepower and whiskey,
an eternity before the bus

chuffed in. How is it that time
is slow and heavy as an elephant
when you're young and impatient to get
to the next second? Now, the merry-
go-round of years, a heartbeat
between Christmases. It's like you
go out a girl who can honky tonk
all night and come home old, smelling
of spiced apples and cat, fat
with memories coding your bones.

Excavating the Past

Recall a place you lived or visited, if only briefly, and use
that as the title of your poem: "Portland, at Dawn 1986,"
for example, or "Honolulu at Happy Hour." Open the
poem by returning to that place in sensory images. Somewhere in the middle of the poem, make a declaration similar
to "How is it" in "Ann Arbor 1974" and let the poem lead
you into some new understanding of the experience.

Works Cited

Frelich, Sarah. "Ann Arbor, 1974." *We*, Harbor Editions, 2021, p. 9.

Otsuka, Julie. *The Swimmers*. Alfred A. Knopf, 2022.

The Outdoor Swimming Society, https://www.
outdoorswimmingsociety.com/about-the-outdoor-swimming-
society/.

Self-Care for the Disabled and/ or Chronically Ill Writer

Jeannine Hall Gailey

PERHAPS YOU, LIKE ME, deal with a disability or chronic illness or, also like me, a combination of both. Since I became a writer twenty-some years ago, I've been diagnosed with a hereditary bleeding disorder, asthma, a genetic primary immune deficiency, terminal liver cancer (now on hold as regular, slow-growing tumors), food allergies, and multiple sclerosis. And they're still testing me for stuff!

Now, Jeannine, (you may be thinking), this is a very serious topic, not the place for humor. And it is! Life-or-death serious. When you are chronically ill or disabled, self-care is a must—not a choice. Neglecting the signals your body is giving you—as I have done when I had, for instance, double pneumonia and went on a work trip anyway—can be fatal. And the last two years have taught us, a little coronavirus—the majority of which are mostly experienced by adults as colds—can cause massive organ failure, long-term disability, and even death, even for people without our health problems.

But just because this is a serious topic doesn't mean we can't have a little fun. So I'm going to give you a list of what not to do as a writer with a disability and/or chronic illness if you're trying to take good care of yourself, the only body you've got, and your career as a writer. And a list of things to do.

What Not to Do

1. *Don't say "yes" to everything.* This one is sort of self-explanatory, but seriously difficult sometimes to live by. Everyone, even "normies" who have no chronic illness or disabilities, is told to make boundaries. For you, this is a must. I am the kind of person who wants to help everyone, fix everyone's problems, go to everyone's readings—but you know what? I can't. I am just one person, and, at that, a person who must take downtime and go to doctor appointments and things like physical therapy. Does it make everyone happy with you all the time? It does not. But just have a "no" stamp ready to go in your mind.

2. *Don't give too much to your job or your volunteer work.* This one is connected to the first, but even if you're volunteering for a noble cause, like curing children's cancer, you cannot afford to do everything people ask you to do. If everyone else at your job is working ninety hours a week, you might want to look for another job, because in reality, they will expect that from you too; that's their culture. Before I became a full-time writer I worked in tech. After I worked as an adjunct. There was a big difference in pay, but one thing was the same: they would have both worked me to death if I was willing.

3. *Don't blow off writer friendships.* I know this one is hard, because of the aforementioned extra taxing work of being a sick or disabled person. It's hard making dates with friends because you're afraid you might encounter stairs you can't take or you'll have to cancel last minute because of a flare-up of your illness. But putting friendships with writers at the top of your to-do list will pay off in multiple ways—it'll encourage you on your own writing journey, you'll stay connected instead of isolating yourself (a big danger for us in the disabled and chronic illness community, especially after the

last two years), and you'll build a network of people you care about who also care about you (ideally—hey, a lot of writers are no treat! So take any toxic narcissists off your writer-friend list. You cannot afford to be with people who take more than they give. The math will not work in your favor.)

4. *Don't blow off sleep and down time.* Scheduling "nothing to do" in your calendar is very important, especially right after or right before things like AWP, a public reading, a root canal, or other stressful life events. More than your friends or family, you may need a day or two to recover from something like a day trip to do a reading or an afternoon of doctor visits and tests. And that's okay. When I was young, I was like "I'll sleep when I'm dead!" But now I know I don't need to rush it—sleep is an important repair mechanism. I'm terrible at this, by the way—I hate down time and always feel the need to be doing something. (When I was still a teen, I bought a book called *When I Relax I Feel Guilty.* I also had an eating disorder and ulcers. Don't be like me as a teen.) Ignoring the need for sleep will just make you feel worse in the long run.

5. *Don't be ashamed of promoting your work however you need to.* I wrote this little book called *PR for Poets* a few years ago (Two Sylvias Press). In it, I talk about how I know it's hard even for completely healthy people to do publicity for their books—especially poets, and especially people who work with small presses. You work all that time on a book, and then when it comes out and the response is a little less than you expected, just remember, this is hard for everyone. It feels overwhelming, and most writers are introverts anyway. So if you need to post on Twitter, do a Zoom reading, or just send out postcards with your book cover, whatever you do, do not feel like you're not doing enough, and certainly don't feel ashamed of doing it. Whatever you need to do, please give yourself some grace.

And here are some Dos

1. *Do be clear about your needs for events.* Ask if there are stairs, if there's a ramp or an elevator, if there will be allergy-friendly food or drinks. Will there be closed-captioning available? Do you need to Zoom in instead of being there in person? Do not be afraid to ask. The downside

of being "too polite" to ask is, if you have a terrible time or get sick or hospitalized because the venue or person didn't think about accessibility, guess what? It will happen to the next person with those issues as well. It doesn't hurt "normies" to think about accessibility once in a while.

2. *Do schedule as much of your life as possible around joy.* I am almost fifty years old, and you know what I wish I'd done more of? Work meetings. Just kidding! I regret not prioritizing joy earlier in my life. If you live for art museums, please make sure and visit the ones in your town. If you love music, going to a concert or an intimate performance will enrich other aspects of your life as well. It is so easy to become—that is, your whole identity becomes—"the sick/disabled person." The way to counter that is just to say: these are the things that bring me joy, even if they're little things—visiting a nearby town's famous ice cream shop, driving a couple of hours to be in a forest or on a beach, or visiting a farmer's market for flowers and fresh fruit. This is how I counter bitterness and its good friend, bitchiness. (And believe me, I have those

days—more than I would like to admit.) Joy! If you don't know yet what gives you joy, because you've been too busy being sick and disabled and a workaholic perfectionist to do anything fun for yourself, explore some things and find out!

3. *Do good things for your body.* Things like feeding it healthy food and getting it outdoors when the weather is appropriate (hey, I know for people with MS this is a tough one—hot weather can put us in bed for days!). Keep an eye on your mental state and see a counselor if you feel too anxious or depressed. Treat your own self like you would your best friend—give her enough water, alone time, vitamin C, sunshine— whatever it is the self needs. Sometimes I think of my body like a really nice but high-maintenance animal, like a fancy horse or special-needs cat. It might be high-strung and needy, but don't treat it badly because of that—you'll get the best response from paying close attention to the treatment your body responds to best. And trust me: ignoring your body is not a good idea in the long run, for you or your writing.

4. *Do share about your health needs.* Share them with your doctor, a friend, a family member, or a counselor. I was horrified reading a recent fiction book about a character who kept passing out from bleeding from endometriosis but literally talked to no one about it, including her parents or a doctor, and broke up with a boyfriend character because she didn't know if she could have kids, without talking to him about whether he even wanted kids. This is a perfect example of how to make your own life more miserable and yourself more isolated! Please do share your condition with trusted and supportive family and friends, and especially with a partner (your relationship should be strong enough to be honest about this kind of stuff, right?). Most of us don't want to admit any vulnerabilities, but I've found that in most cases, people are very supportive—and if they're not, maybe they're not people you want in your life. I mean, give them a chance to show you their best or their worst. (If you are at a job that is not ADA supportive, and I know there are a lot of them, maybe do not share everything with your boss or HR, as they may use that information against you. This has

unfortunately been the case for me at least once
and for friends lots of times. In those cases,
need-to-know basis for info only.)

I hope this has been a helpful essay. I am still learning
about how to best manage my many health problems to
live as full a writing life as possible, and I promise if I learn
any new secrets I will share them as soon as possible. I have
a pretty transparent blog at www.webbish6.com if you want
to follow along the ups and downs of living with MS, a
bleeding disorder, a primary immune deficiency, and some
other stuff. Remember: don't be afraid to ask for help, and
don't hesitate to offer it to others who need it. I'm pretty
sure that will help make the world a better place for everyone with disabilities and chronic illness.

Prompt

Write a fifteen-line poem based on something from your self-care arsenal (or another one you've read about — GOOP stuff always makes me laugh, which can be a great poetry start)—from gardening, to hygge, to crystals, to meditation—whatever your self-care go-to is—write about it from a third person's point of view. Make it humorous, make it scary, make it prophetic—try to make it a little different mood than you might expect for the subject matter.

Dwell

Suzanne Frischkorn

THE FOREST FOLIAGE IS at peak color. Acres of red, orange, and yellow leaves surround our converted barn house and line the roads in corridors. All week I've been distracted by its vivacity. It's not possible to ignore the forest—it's more than half of our town. According to *The Redding Book of Trails*, "It is a forest in which the oak is predominant; red oak, mostly, though black and white and chestnut oaks get mixed in here and there with the hickories, black birch and white ash, dogwood and ironwood, beech, tulip poplar, hemlock, and the maples, both sugar and red" (Redding Land Trust). And it's not possible to ignore that today is too warm for November in New England. Sunny with a clear blue sky, thousands of yellow leaves on the sugar maples, and the windows open to a mild breeze. I can still hear birdsong, though evenings continue to draw in. This is our last autumn in this forest, and I'm overcome with sadness when I remember we're moving to Central New York.

We're about to close on the worst house on the best block. Don't tell the sellers, but I think it's the best house on the best block. It's a ranch home with strong mid-century modern features, it's full of light, and the neighborhood is private. We'll have neighbors, but they won't be visible from the windows because someone had the foresight to plant evergreens on three sides of the property line.

The light is important. Where we dwell makes an impact. Living in the forest for six years has been as restorative as the previous fifteen years we'd lived in a factory town were dispiriting. The village we're moving to is close to my husband's new workplace, but far enough removed that I'll be able to feel removed. As a writer this is the tricky part. How do I stay in the world and retreat from the world to write? How do I master balance?

There was a time when I longed for silence like Mrs. Ramsay in Virginia Woolf's *To the Lighthouse* (43). This was also the time when I felt like a woman in a Loretta Lynn song. I had young children at home, and a freshman in high school. We were living in the depressed factory town, and my husband's commute was soul-killing; we had no friends or extended family nearby. I didn't take care of my physical self at the time, yet I was certain I was caring for my writer self. I rose in the dark to write. I sent my husband and children out of the home on weekends. I wrote with urgency, I published, and I lost some friends along the way. I learned a lot about balance in hindsight.

Those years of urgency and not taking care of my body led to burnout. When my children began school, instead of the uninterrupted hours of writing time I had envisioned, I found myself adrift and without a creative community. I was spent, fallow, drained. I'm embarrassed to tell you how long this lasted. I can tell you I stayed away from my desk too long and it took moving to the forest, the election of a buffoon, and a global pandemic for me to return. I learned to care for my physical self—hydrate, avoid processed foods, regular exercise—yet I still needed to learn how to care for my writer self in a way that was healthy and productive.

Moving from the factory town to a rural landscape in the spring of 2016 helped. I'd never lived in a setting with open space, or a town centered in a forest. I began to meander its trails and found the wonder I'd misplaced. I admired the stones stacked into walls long ago by men clearing the land, and their way with balance. The immovable trees—hundreds of feet tall, transforming each season, limber for bending in the wind, sometimes breaking, falling, and wasting nothing. Providing forage for insects, fungi, and sustenance for those trees still standing. I learned so much about cultivating creativity by observing the forest. Did you know sugar maples can live for three hundred years? They've seen some things. And still, they continue to grow, and reach, and flourish, and replenish.

I was wide open with wonder six months later when the 2016 election results came in. When I think back to that time, I remember my attention. The headlines then changed so rapidly you could almost hear them riffle like the shuffle of playing cards. I could not turn away. I was very much in the world. At some point I felt a need to bear witness, and so I began.

Within four years the world shutting down seemed inevitable.

For someone who sought out solitude and silence, the isolation of a global pandemic imparted how much those states need to be balanced by community and conversations. I found myself dwelling on what I'd do when it was safe to return to public spaces. First I would go to art museums, I decided, yet what I missed most was community with other artists, other makers, other writers. Those were the conversations that nourished me, those were the people creating the art that replenished me. I started the drift away from my creative community before the pandemic; now the world was ending, and I realized I'd drifted too far out. My mortality was showing.

That I'd strayed so far from a creative life is a testament to how easy it is to get caught up in the mundanities of living and the many other obligations demanding our attention. It's important for poets to recognize what nourishes their creativity, prioritize what replenishes it, and respect the time needed to implement it. It's vital for poets to embrace wonder and to cherish their like-minded friends.

The world did not end, and I made efforts to rekindle creative relationships. I renewed my sense of play. I sought "beginner's mind." I took advantage of online classes and Zoom readings. I joined an accountability email group. I joined a hashtag group for other early morning writers. When it was safe to return to public spaces, I met poets for brunch and coffee dates. I took a class on contemporary art at a local museum. I spent a day at sculptor Edward Tufte's farm, another at the Guggenheim to see Kandinsky, and another at the Gardner to see Titian. I meandered through the forest, and I finished a new collection of poems.

When we traveled to Syracuse to look at homes we spent a day touring neighborhoods and suburbs. I was drawn to the village and the homes within it because of the scope of architectural styles, and what it said about the individuality of those who dwelled in them. I learned on our tour that a primeval forest was just a few minutes away—a state park where "[n]early half the park's area is old-growth forest...large specimens of tulip trees, sugar maples, beech, basswood, hemlocks, and white cedars. A grove of trees, lying immediately to the southwest of Round Lake, has been called the Tuliptree Cathedral" (Wikipedia). There was little on the housing market and as the day wore on, I worried we wouldn't find the right home.

I wanted to retain my sense of wonder, a way of being of the world, and a place to feel removed from it. I wanted to live in a home full of light to ward off dark days. I wanted a home that induced calm from an aesthetic sensibility. I wanted a space where I could cultivate and nourish creativity. I wanted an easy commute for my husband and a retreat from the world of work for him as well. I wanted to be close to a forest. No one was more surprised than me when we found it.

I've already connected with some writers in Central New York, and the previous owner of our new home was a doctor who went to art school. He was a passionate pianist and a ceramic artist. I didn't know this when we toured the house, but it's wonderful that I was drawn to a home full of creative energy. A home in a village where I can "dwell in possibility" (Dickinson).

Suzanne Frischkorn

Prompt

Write an ode to the place or space that nourishes your
creative spirit. Choose a word that can be used as a verb
and a noun—use both variations of the word throughout
the poem.

Works Cited

"The Forest-Redding Book of Trails." Redding Land Trust,
    reddingctlandtrust.org/the-forest.

Poetry Foundation. "I Dwell in Possibility – (466) by Emily
    Dickinson." *Poetry Foundation*, 1999, poetryfoundation.org/
    poems/52197/i-dwell-in-possibility-466.

Wikipedia contributors. "Green Lakes State Park." *Wikipedia*, 21
    Oct. 2022, en.wikipedia.org/wiki/Green_Lakes_State_Park.

Woolf, Virginia. "To the Lighthouse." Etext—Opentextbc.ca.
    BCcampus Open Publishing, opentextbc.ca/englishliterature/
    wp-content/uploads/sites/27/2014/10/To-the-Lighthouse-
    Etext-Edited.pdf.

What Punk Rock Taught Me About Self-Care

Mixby Dickon

WE DON'T USUALLY THINK of the punk rock scene when it comes to effective self-care advice. The lyrics of Siouxsie Sioux aren't written in loopy font on inspirational posters. Johnny Rotten sang about his anger and disillusionment with the world and music, but his lyrics never reminded me to drink water. It's a shame that conversations about self-care so often slip into comfortable platitudes: say your affirmations, drink water, practice good hygiene, get sufficient sleep, etc. While these mantras are usually good natured, they often address self-care only in superficial terms.

John Lydon (aka Johnny Rotten) once quipped to an interviewer, "Am I not entitled to do what I want with my own body?" ("10 Times Johnny Rotten Outclassed Interviewers"). Now Lydon has since fallen off of the pedestal that I admittedly built for him, but his talent for shutting down interviews gets to the center of a less superficial pillar of self-care: the art of drawing boundaries. This also became one of the pillars of the punk and post-punk movements that he helped to spearhead. The mohawks, chains, leather, and transgressive lyrics are only on the surface level of punk rock. At its heart are the tenets of freedom of expression, bodily autonomy, subversions of authority, and yes, self-care.

Let me come at this from another angle. I am an intersectional-feminist queer poet who, as one might have already guessed, listens to too much post-punk. I also became the authority figure that I have always railed against when I started teaching English Composition as part of my graduate assistantship—Saint Jimmy save me. In the first week of each class, I set a day aside to talk about self-care and coping mechanisms for my students. Some are pleasantly surprised when I start this talk by telling them that their physical and mental well-being is more important than my class. This is the first boundary that I draw for them.

I then ask them what self-care regimens they have in place to destress during the semester—and I am *very* open to acknowledging that such a day *will* come. Some of them use the usual mantras (which are fine as long as they help!) while others mention personal interests. Listening to music, reading, and watching television are among the most common. I genuinely don't mean for this to be a trick question for my class, but very rarely do they bring up boundaries in this conversation. Self-care can take more than one form and look like a lot of things: eating healthy meals, engaging in personal hobbies, getting exercise, etc. But it can also look like a student prioritizing their comfort, boundaries, and autonomy. I hope to instill this in my students, especially the ones who want to continue writing outside of English Composition.

As writers, our boundaries are important to us. Many of us block off a few hours of every day to work on our craft. We know our bodies and minds. We know when we are most and least productive with our work. We draw this as one of our boundaries and hope that our loved ones will understand and respect that line. In one sense, writing is a quintessential act of autonomy. As writers, we are in control of not just the words on the page but also the stories that they tell. Our work has the potential to be a safe space, to be unapologetically authentic to ourselves. It's even up to us to decide if we are ready to write about painful experiences and trauma.

Let's go back to punk rock. Poly Styrene (born Marianne Elliott-Said), the front person for English punk band X-Ray Spex, once said, "I think it [punk] should be a form of self-expression. Everyone should just wear what they want to wear and not have to go to certain shops and buy certain things" (Poly Styrene Interview, 1978). As both artists and as humans, writers can engage in a more complex form of self-care by finding ways to be themselves unapologetically. As writers, one of the hardest things to develop is our voice. The spark of individuality that makes us ourselves on the page can be illusive. In a society that compels individuals to conform to a mythical norm, taking Poly Styrene's advice is both an act of self-care and an act of rebellion. Styrene's words can also remind us as writers to protect our voices.

Nowhere is the importance of protecting the value of our time and voices more significant than in an MFA workshop. While not all writers complete such a program, those who have done so know the combination of excitement and anxiety that comes with having all eyes in the room on their work. While I would not recommend swearing and leaving the classroom in the spirit of Johnny Rotten canceling an interview in progress, that detached self-protection can serve a writer well when listening to criticism of their work. I do not mean to say that workshop critique should be ignored, especially when multiple structural, stylistic issues receive repeated feedback from more than one person. When feedback gets too close to the voice and character of the work, this is where drawing boundaries can be an important act of self-care, and the standoffish individualism of Kurt Cobain or Johnny Rotten can have a beneficial effect on the mental health (and sanity) of the writer. Substantial effort goes into developing our voices as writers. If we reach that point where we sound like ourselves on the page, that characteristic of our writing deserves to be protected.

Self-care may be hard to find in post-punk spaces, but that doesn't mean it isn't there. Self-care is so often focused on the same mantras that fail to get to the complexity of mental health issues that both writers and nonwriters regularly navigate. At least one in five adults suffer from a mental illness (National Institute of Mental Health). Some of them have already cleaned their rooms, changed their diets, and changed their activity levels. If none of that works, more nuanced measures will be needed. It's a cruel injustice to tell someone who is drowning to drink more water.

Yes: in self-care it is important to treat our bodies with dignity and respect—whatever that means for each individual. Punk rock teaches both writers and nonwriters a more nuanced way of navigating self-care, a way that includes an important element of psychic self-defense. Self-care is protecting our voices, our identities, and what makes us unique. Sometimes, self-care is unhooking the microphone and leaving in the middle of an interview.

> "I don't give a shit what you think…
>   I don't try to impress anybody but myself"
> —Johnny Rotten Interview, 1977.

Prompt

Think of a figure of pop culture that has influenced you
personally or artistically. Alternatively, instead of an individual, this can be a movement in any art form including
music, film, visual art, digital art, or literature—or anything else that I forgot to list! Once you have your influence
chosen, write either an ekphrastic or confessional poem in
which you channel the energies and emotions of that individual or movement. No matter which form in which you
choose to write, include at least one quote from that individual or an artist in the movement. This can appear either
in the body of the poem or as an epigraph. If you choose
an epigraph, look for clever ways to include the words of
the quote in the poem. Include at least one concrete image
to anchor the reader.

Works Cited

Author unknown. "Mental Illness" *National Institute of Mental
    Health*. January 2022. https://www.nimh.nih.gov/health/
    statistics/mental-illness.

Elliott-Said, Marianne. "Poly Styrene Interview 1978." *YouTube*,
    uploaded by chatham43, March 3, 2009. https://youtu.be/A_
    R2UrRME_E.

"Johnny Rotten 1977 Interview." *YouTube*, uploaded by eversore, October 3, 2013. https://www.youtube.com/watch?v=nMBX7wxoNGw.

Lydon, John. "10 Times Johnny Rotten Outclassed Interviewers." *YouTube*, uploaded by Livewire, March 19, 2018. https:// https://www.youtube.com/watch?v=EcZne8YKgGY.

"Productive" Poet

What Can "Writing" Look Like?

Emily Corwin

WRITING DOES NOT ALWAYS *look* like writing. The immaculate picture of The Writer intently sitting down to work, with a gorgeous latte, their head flanked by verdant, hanging plants and an organized desk, cast glowingly in morning sun: this is, of course, a fiction. As Anne Lamott says in "Shitty First Drafts":

> People tend to look at successful writers ... and think that they sit down at their desks every morning feeling like a million dollars, feeling great about who they are and how much talent they have and what a great story they have to tell.... But this is just the fantasy of the uninitiated. (21)

The writing process becomes particular to each writer, like a favorite pair of jeans worn over many years. When teaching writing, I try not to prescribe any one process to my students, but instead introduce possibilities, strategies, methods for generating work. As for myself, I have certain modes that work within my disposition, specifically with my anxiety.

My anxiety disorder feeds on particular subjects: body horror, interpersonal conflict, the internet, body horror and the internet, interpersonal conflict and the internet. Being in a body is unavoidable, and conflict with other humans is also unavoidable, and so, too, is the internet. While I can't control that I exist in a body (one that needs connection), I *can,* to some extent, limit my time online (sometimes successfully, sometimes not). The babble and shine of screens becomes too much for me. After scrolling on the eternal loop, I feel ill, as with motion sickness. When I need to pause, I make myself essentially an island. I shut down my phone, place it in another room. I close my door, dim the lights, turn on the box fan: my own sense-deprivation chamber. When I'm in my room, shut off from cyber and non-cyber worlds, I feel safer, calmer, less afraid of myself and others. In my enclosed space, I become unburdened, become more able to rest, to read, to think, to write.

My writing may look like a lot of nothing. It is contemplation, introspection, being idle, seemingly wasting the afternoon away. I make coffee, I read *Cosmo,* I text my sister,

I get out my journal and list items in my room that are pink. When I was in graduate school, I produced writing like a factory machine, cranking poems out without much thought or time or patience. When I wasn't in class, I was in coffee shops making more poems, restless and rushed and halfhearted, more focused on generating poems than on their craft. Although I still have some affection for that early work, I see its impatience and anxiety, its eagerness to be made and done with. Once I graduated, without the catalyst of the workshop atmosphere, I slowed down so much that I worried I would never write the same again. And I haven't written with the desperation I did before; I am glad for it. Once I was a newly minted MFA, I don't think I wrote a new poem for a year afterward, and my "productivity" continued sporadically. And now, four years later, I write in my journal daily, but my writing projects seem to have a "long game" in mind. When I sit down to write a poem or a piece of an essay, I see a book, a collection, an extensive work that will take years to create. I write for a while and stop, go shopping or go to work, spend time with my family, take a road trip; then weeks later, I pick up where I left off with another piece to add (like with this very essay that you are reading). I like this process: it requires more intention than how I wrote as a younger person.

For me now, writing looks like this: shadowy, white noise, relaxed and slow, lying on my side or propped up with a pillow. I do my best "writing" like this: jotting ideas down, making lists, reading poems by friends, daydreaming, taking my medication, drifting off, coming back gently to an idea. Instead of hurrying myself through a process, I have developed this care towards myself and my words. It doesn't feel "productive" or like "work"; it feels like peace.

Prompt

Choose a fun word or phrase composed of an unusual mix of letters: "chrysanthemum" or "strawberry daiquiri" or "Lavender Haze" (if you're a Taylor Swift fan). Then, create a word bank using only the letters in your word or phrase (yes, you can repeat letters). Finally, compose a poem using (if you can) only the words in your word bank. Not only is this constraint a relaxing activity (at least it is for me), but it also creates a cohesive soundscape for your poem.

Works Cited

Lamott, Anne. *Bird by Bird: Some Instructions on Writing and Life*. Anchor Books, 1995.

Acknowledgments

THE EDITORS WISH TO send their profound gratitude to the University of Akron Press and Akron Series in Contemporary Poetics for support of this volume.

To our ten contributors: we are overwhelmed with appreciation for all that you've shared. Special thanks to Lee Ann Roripaugh for the "mollusk without a shell" part of this essay collection's title.

We are grateful to Rhye Pirie for creating the gorgeous art on the cover of *A Mollusk Without a Shell*. Thank you for bringing our vision of the book to life, Rhye.

Sincere thanks to colleagues, friends, and family who helped support this project or helped support us as we worked on this project: Chad Barbour, Eleanor Barbour, Amy Freels, John Gallaher, Julie Gammon, Brittany

LaPointe, Thea Ledendecker, Jordan McNeil, Jon Miller, Eric Morris, Emily Price, Nick Sturm, Gabi Thompson, Gale Marie Thompson, and Ray Thompson.

Love to our many dear companion animals who provided comfort and cheer during the time that we worked on this project: Blanche, Henri, Jacques, Lulu, and Penelope, and Bruno, Daphne, Logan, Lucy, Percy, Septimus, and Zooey.

This book is dedicated to our students, with thanks for their constant inspiration.

Contributors

Kelli Russell Agodon's newest book is *Dialogues with Rising Tides* from Copper Canyon Press. She is the cofounder of Two Sylvias Press where she works as an editor and book cover designer. She teaches at Pacific Lutheran University's low-res MFA program, the Rainier Writing Workshop. She lives in a sleepy seaside town in Washington State on traditional lands of the Chimacum, Coast Salish, S'Klallam, and Suquamish people, where she is an avid paddleboarder and hiker. Kelli is currently part of a project between local land trusts and artists to help raise awareness for the preservation of land, ecosystems, and biodiversity called Writing the Land. www.agodon.com / www.twosylviaspress.com

Abayomi Animashaun is an immigrant from Nigeria. He is the author of three poetry collections and editor of three anthologies. He is an assistant professor of English at the University of Wisconsin, Oshkosh, and a poetry editor at *The Comstock Review*.

Emily Corwin's writing has appeared in *Salamander*, *Black Warrior Review*, *Passages North*, *DIAGRAM*, *Ninth Letter*, *New South*, and elsewhere. Her books include *tenderling* (Stalking Horse Press, 2018), *sensorium* (University of Akron Press, 2020), and *Marble Orchard* (University of Akron Press, 2023). She lives and works in Michigan with her love-person, Joe, and her very pretty cat, Soup.

Mixby Dickon (she/they) is a nonbinary poet and a self-described anarchist. When they are not reading their work to the feral animals under their bedroom window, they are living their best life with their chosen family: their partner Tab and a beautiful tortie cat named Harley. She is a recent graduate of the NEOMFA creative writing program.

Sarah Freligh is the author of four books, including *Sad Math*, winner of the 2014 Moon City Press Poetry Prize and the 2015 Whirling Prize from the University of Indianapolis, and *We*, published by Harbor Editions in early 2021. Recent work has appeared in the *Cincinnati Review* miCRo series, *SmokeLong Quarterly*, *Wigleaf*, *Fractured*

Lit, and in the anthologies *New Micro: Exceptionally Short Fiction* (Norton, 2018), *Best Microfiction* (2019–22) and *Best Small Fictions 2022*. Among her awards are poetry fellowships from the National Endowment for the Arts and the Saltonstall Foundation for the Arts.

Suzanne Frischkorn's fourth book of poems, *Whipsaw*, is forthcoming in 2024 from Anhinga Press. Her most recent book, *Fixed Star* (JackLeg Press, 2022), was a finalist for the 2022 Foreword INDIES Award. She is the recipient of The Writer's Center Emerging Writers Fellowship for her book, *Lit Windowpane*, the Aldrich Poetry Award for her chapbook, *Spring Tide*, selected by Mary Oliver, an Individual Artist Fellowship from the Connecticut Commission on Culture & Tourism, and a 2023 *SWWIM* Residency Award at The Betsy. Her poems are forthcoming in *Latino Poetry: The Library of America Anthology*, edited by Rigoberto González (Library of America 2024), *Salamander*, *South Dakota Review*, and elsewhere. She is an editor at *$ – Poetry Is Currency*, and serves on the *Terrain. org* editorial board.

Jeannine Hall Gailey is a poet with multiple sclerosis who served as the second Poet Laureate of Redmond, Washington. She's the author of six books of poetry: *Becoming the Villainess*, *She Returns to the Floating World*, *Unexplained Fevers*, *The Robot Scientist's Daughter*, *Field Guide to the End of the World*, winner of the Moon City Press Book

Prize and the Elgin Award, and *Flare, Corona* from BOA Editions. She has a BS in Biology and an MA in English from the University of Cincinnati, and an MFA from Pacific University. Her work has appeared in *The American Poetry Review*, *Ploughshares*, and *Poetry*. Her website is www.webbish6.com. Twitter and Instagram: @webbish6.

Charles Jensen (he/him) is the author of the poetry collection *Nanopedia* and six chapbooks of poems. His third collection, *Instructions between Takeoff and Landing*, was published by the University of Akron Press in 2022. He received the 2020 OutWrite Nonfiction Chapbook Award for *Cross-Cutting*, a diptych of essays that hybridize memoir and film criticism. The City of Los Angeles Department of Cultural Affairs designated him a 2019–2020 Cultural Trailblazer, and he is the recipient of the 2018 Zócalo Poetry Prize, a Dorothy Sargent Rosenberg Prize, the 2007 Frank O'Hara Chapbook Award, and an Artist's Project Grant from the Arizona Commission on the Arts. His poetry has appeared in *American Poetry Review*, *Crab Orchard Review*, *The Journal*, *New England Review*, and *Prairie Schooner*, and essays have appeared in *45th Parallel*, *American Literary Review*, and *The Florida Review*. He founded the online poetry magazine *LOCUSPOINT*, which explored creative work on a city-by-city basis. He hosts *The Write Process*, a podcast in which one writer tells the story of crafting one work from concept to completion, and with Jovonnie Anaya co-hosts *You Wanna Be on Top?*, an episode-by-episode retrospective of *America's Next Top Model.* He lives in Los Angeles and directs the Writers' Program at UCLA Extension.

Lee Ann Roripaugh's fifth volume of poetry, *tsunami vs. the fukushima 50* (Milkweed Editions, 2019), was named a "Best Book of 2019" by the New York Public Library, selected as a poetry Finalist in the 2020 Lambda Literary Awards, cited as a Society of Midland Authors 2020 Honoree in Poetry, and was named one of the "50 Must-Read Poetry Collections in 2019" by Book Riot. She is the author of four other volumes of poetry: *Dandarians* (Milkweed, Editions, 2014), *On the Cusp of a Dangerous Year* (Southern Illinois University Press, 2009), *Year of the Snake* (Southern Illinois University Press, 2004), and *Beyond Heart Mountain* (Penguin, 1999). She was named winner of the Association of Asian American Studies Book Award in Poetry/Prose for 2004 and a 1998 winner of the National Poetry Series. The South Dakota State Poet Laureate from 2015–2019, Roripaugh is a professor of English at the University of South Dakota, where she serves as Director of Creative Writing and Editor-in-Chief of *South Dakota Review.* Roripaugh served as one of the jurors for the 2021 Pulitzer Prize in Poetry and was appointed as the Mary Rogers Field and Marion Field-McKenna Distinguished Professor of Creative Writing at DePauw University for spring 2022.

Jenny Sadre-Orafai is the author of *Paper Cotton Leather* and *Malak,* and the co-author of *Book of Levitations.* Her fourth poetry collection, *Dear Outsiders*, was published by the University of Akron Press. Her prose has appeared in *The Rumpus*, *Fourteen Hills*, *The Los Angeles Review*, and others. She co-founded *Josephine Quarterly* and teaches creative writing at Kennesaw State University.

About the Editors

Julie Brooks Barbour's most recent poetry collection is *Haunted City* (Kelsay Books, 2017). Her work has appeared in *South Dakota Review*, *Glass: A Journal of Poetry*, *Whale Road Review*, *Escape Into Life*, *Moon City Review*, *Gone Lawn*, *Menacing Hedge*, and *Allium, A Journal of Poetry and Prose*. She teaches writing at Lake Superior State University where she edits the journal *Border Crossing*.

Mary Biddinger's most recent poetry collections are *Partial Genius: Prose Poems* and *Department of Elegy*, both with Black Lawrence Press. Her poems have appeared in a variety of journals, including *A Dozen Nothing*, *The Laurel Review*, and *Pithead Chapel*, and have been featured on *Poetry Daily* and *The Slowdown*. Biddinger's flash fiction has been published in *Always Crashing*, *DIAGRAM*, *Gone Lawn*, and *Southern Indiana Review*. She teaches creative writing at the University of Akron and in the NEOMFA program.